EUDIST PRAYERBOOK SERIES:
VOLUME 1

HEART OF THE HOLY FAMILY
A MANUAL OF PRAYER
by St. John Eudes

Originally published as Congregation de Jèsus et Marie
Manuel de Prière (Extraits) Nantes, Cid Éditions, 1989

IMPRIMI POTEST:
Paris, December 30, 1988
M. LeBourg, CJM
Provincial

IMPRIMATUR:
Paris, January 9, 1989
M. Vidal, V.É

Translated by
Steven S. Marshall

Cover image: a 40 ton marble statue of St. John Eudes in St. Peter's Basilica. Carved in 1932 by Silvio Silva, this is one of 39 large statues around the Basilica's nave and transepts honoring the founders of great religious orders.

ISBN: 978-0-9979114-0-4

Copyright ©2018, by
The Eudists – Congregation of Jesus and Mary, US Region

Published by

EUDIST
PRESS

744 Sonrisa Street
Solana Beach, CA 92075
www.eudistsusa.org

THE
EUDISTS
CONGREGATION OF
JESUS AND MARY

Table of Contents

Note: Some prayer titles are in Latin, but all the prayers are in English.

Introduction

Everything in this book points to the Incarnation. The God who made the universe entering into human reality: A God with hands, arms, eyes and ears; family members, suffering and pain; A God who did not come in overwhelming power, but in meekness and humility. It is in flesh, suffering, and humility that He laid the foundation for Christian community.

The prayers in this booklet have been used by bishops, seminary professors, missionaries, and laity from all walks of life, to deepen their relationship with God.

Within the book, you will find litanies, written to be prayed in two voices, alternating like a heartbeat. You will find passages from scripture, rearranged into poetry that can make your heart sing. While the titles of the prayers are presented in Latin, the prayers themselves are given in English.

They were composed by St. John Eudes.

In 17th century France, St. John Eudes lived during a "mystical invasion" of the Church. His seminary education was an immersion in spiritual masters like Saints Ignatius of Loyola, Theresa of Avila, and Francis de Sales. After ordination, he led a wave of "new evangelization" bringing fervor and faith back to a church sorely in need. This booklet collects the essentials of his spirituality, for use on a daily basis.

Behind it all is a man burning with desire, longing to give his heart to Christ just as fully as Mary did. To him, Mary's "yes" to God went far beyond her *fiat* on the day of the Annunciation. As the prototype of all Christians, she united her heart so closely to that of Jesus, that they had only one heart between them. With this insight, St. John Eudes became one of the first to spread devotion to the Sacred and Immaculate Hearts. With his help, we pray that you too can fall ever more deeply in love with our Lord and His mother.

May God bless and Mary keep you!

Steve Marshall MA
US Region Secretary
The Eudists – Congregation of Jesus & Mary

To Prepare for Prayer

The leader of prayer reads each phrase aloud. It is followed by a moment of silence, so each individual can personally converse with God as indicated.

1. Let us adore God the Father.
   Let us humble ourselves before Him.
   Let us offer Him our spirit and our heart, with the desire to live this time of prayer to the fullest, solely for love of Him.

2. Let us renounce our own selves, and offer ourselves to our Lord Jesus Christ, that we may offer our prayers in His Spirit.

3. Let us ask the Virgin Mary and all the saints to help us in our prayer, and to join us to their eternal prayer before God.

To Conclude a Time of Prayer

1. Let us thank God for the grace which He has given us.
   Let us ask His pardon for our moments of negligence;
   let us ask our Lord Jesus Christ to make up for these faults and to be, Himself, our eternal prayer to His Father.

2. Let us gather up the grace of this time, the best of what God has given us in prayer, so that this grace may come to life in us.

3. Recognizing that we cannot reach perfection on our own, let us place our trust, let us place all our trust in the mercy of God. Let us ask the Virgin Mary and all the saints to continue our prayer and to join us to theirs which they make eternally before God.

4 Let us examine our lives, trying to see ways in which we may live more faithfully before God. Let us think in particular of the essentials of community life: humility, obedience, charity, and meekness.

Let us pray,

Lord Jesus, may the action of Your Spirit seize our spirits and our bodies; so that His influence, not our own sentiments, may always rule within us. You who live and reign forever and ever.

Amen.

LITANIES

Ave Cor

Salutation to the Heart of Jesus & Mary
If said in community, pray in two voices, alternating like a heartbeat.

Hail, Heart most holy,
    Hail, Heart most meek,
Hail, Heart most humble,
    Hail, Heart most pure,
Hail, Heart most devout,
    Hail, Heart most wise,
Hail, Heart most patient,
    Hail, Heart most obedient,
Hail, Heart most vigilant
    Hail, Heart most faithful
Hail, Heart most blessed,
    Hail, Heart most merciful.
Hail, most loving Heart of Jesus and Mary.

We adore You,
    We praise You,
We glorify You,
    We give You thanks;
We love You,
    With all our heart,
With all our soul,
    With all our strength.
We offer You our heart,
    We give it to You,
We consecrate it to You,
    We sacrifice it to You;
Receive and possess it totally.

Purify it,
    Enlighten it,
Sanctify it;

ALL:
In it, live and reign,
now and forever,
world without end.
Amen.

Ave Maria, Filia Dei Patris

Salutation to the Virgin Mary

If said in community, pray in two voices, alternating like a heartbeat.

Hail Mary, daughter of God the Father,
    Hail Mary, mother of God the Son,
Hail Mary, spouse of the Holy Spirit,
    Hail Mary, temple of the whole Divinity.
Hail Mary, immaculate lily of the resplendent and ever-peaceful
Trinity;
    Hail Mary, radiant rose of heavenly fragrance;
Hail Mary, virgin of virgins, faithful virgin, chosen by the King of
heaven to bear Him to the world and to nourish Him at your
breast;
    Hail Mary, queen of martyrs, whose soul was pierced by a sword
    of sorrows;
Hail Mary, queen of the universe, to whom has been given all power
in heaven and earth,
    Hail Mary, queen of my heart, my mother, my life, my sweetness,
    and my dearest hope;
Hail Mary, mother most lovable;
    Hail Mary, mother most admirable;
Hail Mary, mother of mercy;
    Hail Mary, full of grace, the Lord is with you,
Blessed are you among women,
    And blessed be the fruit of your womb Jesus;
    And blessed be your spouse St. Joseph;
    And blessed be your father St. Joachim;
    And blessed be your mother St. Anne;
    And blessed be your son St. John;
    And blessed be your angel St. Gabriel;
    And blessed be the Eternal Father who chose you;
    And blessed be the Divine Son who loved you;
    And blessed be the Holy Spirit who espoused you;
    And blessed be forever all those who bless and love you
    Amen.

Ave Joseph

Salutation to St. Joseph

If said in community, pray in two voices, alternating like a heartbeat.

Hail Joseph, image of God the Father,
   Hail Joseph, father of God the Son,
Hail Joseph, temple of the Holy Spirit,
   Hail Joseph, beloved of the Holy Trinity.
Hail Joseph, most faithful helper in the work of God,
   Hail Joseph, most worthy spouse of the Virgin Mother,
Hail Joseph, father of all the faithful,
   Hail Joseph, guardian of holy virgins,
Hail Joseph, most attentive to interior silence,
   Hail Joseph, most loving of holy poverty,
Hail Joseph, example of meekness and patience,
   Hail Joseph, mirror of humility and obedience.

Blessed are you
   among all men,
And blessed be your eyes,
   which have seen what you have seen.
And blessed be your ears,
   which have heard what you have heard.
And blessed be your hands,
   which have touched the Word Incarnate.
And blessed be your arms,
   which have carried Him who carries all things.
And blessed be your bosom,
   where the Son of God most sweetly rested.
And blessed be your heart,
   burning with the most ardent love for Him.
And blessed be the Eternal Father,
   who chose you,
And blessed be the Son,
   who loved you,

And blessed be the Holy Spirit
    who sanctified you,
And blessed be Mary, your wife,
    who loved you as a spouse and a brother,
And blessed be the Angel
    who protected you,
And blessed be forever
    all those who bless & love you.

    Amen.

A statue of St. John Eudes in
St. Peter's Basilica in Rome

Magnificat of St. John Eudes

Hymn of Praise and Thanksgiving to The Heart of Jesus and Mary for Countless Gifts Received

My soul glorifies the admirable heart of Jesus & Mary, My spirit rejoices in this great Heart which is mine!

Yes, Jesus and Mary have given me their Heart, so that I may live in nothing but in their love.

R\. We praise You infinitely for Your indescribable love!
Your Heart of goodness has done wondrous things for me; You have taken me for Yourself since my mother's womb.

The abyss of my misery called out to the abyss of Your mercy. **R\.** Your most sweet Heart has always surrounded me with its sweetest blessings. I was sheltered in the shadow of Your hand, cared for as the apple of Your eye. **R\.**

You chose me to be Your priest; You raised me to sit with the princes of Your people; You placed Your words in my mouth and made my speech like a two-edged sword. **R\.**

You have made me die, You have made me live, You are with me in all my ways. You have been the enemy of my enemies, and delivered me from all my trials **R\.**

O most loving Heart, source of all goodness, You have given me gifts without measure! To You all praise, all love, and all glory! May every mouth sing Your praise, and every heart cherish You! **R\.**

May Your glory sing out in Your mercy, in the wonders of Your love. May You be eternally blessed, praised and glorified for Your great deeds. **R\.**

Let us pray,

Oh Great Heart, may the Father of Mercies be mindful of Your sacrifice, may He accomplish all Your desires!

O Heart of Jesus, on the Cross You were broken in love and suffering for us. May our hearts be consumed in the fire of Your love until the end of time!

O Heart of Mary, pierced by the sword of sorrow, grant that our hearts may also be pierced by the love which comes from God!

O Heart of Jesus and Mary, furnace of love, may our hearts blaze in Your warmth forever.

May they die in Your flames and may they be one heart with the Heart of Jesus and Mary forever!

Glory to the Father, and to the Son, and to the Holy Spirit...

PRAYERS FOR
VARIOUS
OCCASIONS

Prayer Before Studying

Send Your Wisdom from Your Holy Heaven and from the throne of Your Majesty that She may labor with me, so I may know what is acceptable to You.

And who shall know Your thoughts, unless You give them wisdom, and send Your Holy Spirit from above?

> Give me understanding and I will search for Your Law.

Give me Wisdom, Lord, Who sits by Your throne, and do not cast me out from among Your children.

> Give me understanding and I will search for Your Law.

For I am Your servant, a weak creature, and I fall short of understanding Your judgment and laws.

> Give me understanding and I will search for Your law. And I will keep it with all my heart.

Glory to the Father…

> Give me understanding and I will search for Your law. And I will keep it with all my heart.

Amen.

Prayer Before Meals

O my God,
there are many people who have nothing to eat,
and yet they have not offended You as much as I.
Still, in the extravagance of Your love, You have given this meal to us.
Let us share it in the same spirit of love with which you shared
Your meals on earth, and may each bite be an act of praise and
worship to our Heavenly Father.

OR:

Whether you eat or drink,
whatever you do,
do everything for the glory of God
and in the name of our Lord Jesus Christ.
Amen.

Christus Jesus

Jesus Christ, meek and humble of heart, by the immense charity with
which He has loved us, humbled Himself, made Himself obedient
even unto death on a Cross. Let us live, therefore, in humility,
obedience, charity, and meekness.

ALL:
Amen. Amen.
Yes, Lord Jesus.
By Your grace and for the glory of Your name.
Amen.

Benedictum Sit Cor

Blessed be the most loving Heart
and the most sweet Name
of our Lord Jesus Christ,
and of His mother,
the most glorious Virgin Mary,
for ever and ever.
Amen.

Jesu, Vivens in Maria

Jesus living in Mary, come and live in Your family,
    in the holiness of Your Spirit,
    in the fullness of Your might,
    in the perfection of Your ways,
    in the truth of Your virtues,
    in the communion of Your mysteries.
Subdue every hostile power of our heart, in Your Spirit, for the glory
of God the Father.
Amen.

Benediction

May the Virgin Mary
bless us and keep us
with her Divine Son, Jesus. Amen.

For an Assembly

God of power and mercy, in Your inexhaustible love, You fill those who implore You far beyond what they merit or desire. You who have said "If two or three are gathered in My name, there I am in their midst," we ask You to multiply in us the acts of Your mercy.

Look upon us gathered in Your name. With the prayers of blessed Mary, ever virgin, of St. Gabriel, St. Joseph, St. John the Evangelist, St. John Eudes, and all the angels and saints, pour out in our hearts the light and power of Your Spirit, so that we may know the designs of Your will and accomplish what is pleasing to You, with a loving heart and a willing spirit.

Through Jesus Christ, our Lord. Amen

Christus Jesus Dominus Factus

[Traditionally, this prayer has been used to conclude times of meditation, especially when done in community.]

Christ Jesus was made, by God, our salvation, our justification, and our sanctification. He died for us, so that the living might live, not for themselves but for Him who died and rose again in their name.

V\. We desire Lord Jesus
R\. That You reign over us!

Let us pray: God of power and compassion, destroy totally within us anything which is is opposed to You. Put forth Your strength and take possession of our hearts and bodies to establish perfectly in us the reign of Your Love.

Lord Jesus, through the intercession of the Blessed Mary ever virgin, of St. Gabriel, St. Joseph, St. John the Evangelist, St. John Eudes our father, and of all the saints, protect this family, which is Yours, from every evil, we beg You. In Your goodness, defend us from the snares of the enemy, You who live and reign for ever and ever. Amen.

Evening Prayer

The leader of prayer reads each phrase aloud. It is followed by a moment of silence so each individual can personally converse with God as indicated.

Let us adore God. Let us thank Him for our lives and and for all creation.

✝

Let us adore our Lord Jesus Christ as our Judge; let us ask Him to help us recognize our sins. Let us examine ourselves in what we have done today, thinking particularly of the demands of community life: humility, obedience, charity and meekness.

✝

Let us ask God for contrition. Let us give ourselves to our Lord Jesus Christ to enter into His own spirit of penitence. Let us renounce our sins for love of Him. Let us offer to God the love which Jesus bears for His Father, both in Himself and in all the members of His body.

✝

Let us ask the Virgin Mary and all the saints to obtain for us pardon for our faults and a true conversion.

✝

Let us offer to God the rest which we are about to take, in honor of, and union with the rest which our Lord and His Mother took during their earthly life.

✝

Let us try to end our day in the state in which we would like to be at the hour of our death. Let us give ourselves to our Lord Jesus Christ to enter into the dispositions with which He embraced His death.

SPECIAL DAYS
FOR THE
EUDIST FAMILY

A certain number of these dates were important to St. John Eudes because of the opportunity they offer for spiritual renewal. Others mark particular events which invite us to thanksgiving. For us, each one can be a call to reinvigorate our desire to contemplate Jesus Christ in all the states of His life, to commune with His mysteries, and to give ourselves to His Spirit in order to continue His life and his virtues, "until Christ is formed in us." (Gal. 4:19)

Christmas

During every day of this season, we are invited to contemplate Jesus in the mystery of His infancy. Here is an exercise to help us in that pursuit:

> *Lord Jesus, for love of us, You willed not only to become man, but a tiny infant. Grant that we may venerate this most humble state, into which You emptied Yourself. Grant us the wisdom of Your spirit of childhood. Help us imitate the virtues of Your childhood: innocence and simplicity, purity, sweetness, humility, obedience and charity. Thus, like newborns, we will desire the true spiritual milk, we will learn from You to be meek and humble of heart, and in our smallness before Your face, we may follow You in our little way on earth and may glorify You in Your greatness in heaven. Amen.*

January 9

On this day in 1826, the 26th General Assembly of the CJM, held at Rennes and presided by Fr. Blanchard, reestablished the Congregation of Jesus and Mary after it was destroyed by the French Revolution.

January 16-21

St. John Eudes asked that during these days our prayer be full of thanksgiving for the gift God gave us by calling us to life, both in our birth and in our baptism. The "Exercises to celebrate the anniversary of our Baptism" from St. John Eudes' *Kingdom of Jesus* may be useful to commemorate these days properly.

January 22

On the feast of the Marriage of Mary and Joseph, we also commemorate the dedication of the Congregation, in 1644, to "the divine community of Jesus, Mary and Joseph, who we must consider as the example, model and rule of our Congregation, and which we must live as the image and likeness."

February 8

On this date in 1648, St. John Eudes became the first person in history to celebrate the feast of the Heart of Mary. This Mass and Liturgy of the Hours which he composed has been used around the world ever since. The celebration took place in the Diocese of Autun. Two years later, in the same diocese, St. Margaret Mary Alacoque was born.

> *Father in Heaven, You have willed that Your only Son live and reign in the Heart of the Virgin Mary. Grant that we may always accomplish Your will with love and with all our heart. Thus may we never have but one heart among ourselves and with You.*

March 25

For St. John Eudes, this day was a celebration of the Incarnation and of the Priesthood at the same time. On this day in 1643, he also founded our Congregation. This is the occasion when we are invited to renew our promises of incorporation or association to the CJM.

Renewal of Incorporation Promises:

In the name of the Father, Son and Holy Spirit I renew before You, oh my Lord Jesus, in the presence of Mary Your Mother and all the saints, the promise I made when, through Your mercy, I was incorporated into [associated with] this Congregation; there to live and die, to serve and glorify You as perfectly as possible, through Your grace, in renouncing my own will to follow Yours, of which the will of the superiors and constitutions of this Congregation will be the sign for me.

I beg You, Jesus, to grant me the grace to live this, and I entrust myself to the prayer of the Virgin Mary, of St. Joseph, of St. Gabriel, of St. John the Evangelist, of St. John Eudes, and of all the saints.

Amen.

Easter

A prayer to unite ourselves to the Pascal mystery celebrated during these days:

> *Lord Jesus Christ, true God and life eternal, in Your indescribable mercy You have willed to suffer death on the Cross and to rise again on the third day. You did this so the living may live no longer for themselves, but for Him who died and was raised for them.*
>
> *Grant that the image of Your death and resurrection be so present in us that we place all our pride in Your cross and that, dead to sin, crucified to the world, renouncing ourselves, we may live forever in You and for You.*

April 24

On this day in 1868 St. Mary Euphrasia was born to eternal life. She began her life as a religious in the Sisters of Our Lady of Charity, the first order founded by St. John Eudes, and went on to found the Good Shepherd Sisters, which spread around the world under her guidance. These two religious orders were joyfully reunited into one in 2014.

May 31

This was the day, in 1925, when St. John Eudes was canonized by Pope Pius XI. St. John Vianney was also canonized on this date.

August 19

In Caen, on this day in 1680, St. John Eudes entered into the light of God. Together with the Eudist family and the whole Church, let us pray the opening prayer from the mass celebrating his life both on earth and in heaven:

> *Lord our God, in an admirable way, You chose the priest St John Eudes to proclaim the incomparable riches of Christ. Grant that, by his example and prayer, we may grow in knowledge of You and live faithfully in the light of the Gospel.*

September 2-3

During the Reign of Terror in 1792, over 1,500 priests and religious were executed as enemies of the Revolutionary Government of France. A new law required them to reject the authority of the pope and swear allegiance to the government instead. They refused.

During a two-day period known as the Semptember Massacre, 191 priests were killed. Their names were recorded at the time which allowed them each to be beatified in 1926. Among these blessed martyrs are three Eudists: François-Louis Hébert, François Lefranc and Pierre-Claude Pottier.

October 20

On this date in 1672, St. John Eudes became the first person in history to celebrate the feast of the Heart of Jesus. This Mass and Liturgy of the Hours which he composed has been used around the world ever since.

> *Lord, Father of mercies, in Your goodness without measure You have given us the loving Heart of Your beloved Son. Grant that our hearts may be united so closely among ourselves and with His own, that our love for You may become perfect.*

November 13-20

On the 19th of this month, the feast of Jesus' priesthood is traditionally celebrated, along with that of all the saintly priests and levites. St. John Eudes recommended that these days be spent contemplating the priesthood of Jesus Christ, in which we are given a share. Let us pray together for our priests:

> *Lord Jesus, awaken in Your Church the Spirit which animated the apostles and so many holy priests. Fill us with the same Spirit, so that we may know how to love what they loved and carry out what they teach. Amen.*

November 14

This was the birthday of St. John Eudes in 1601. To him, more important than his birthday was the celebration of his baptism, which was two days later.

November 21

On this feast of the Presentation of Mary, St. John Eudes invited the priests of his Congregation to renew the promises of celibacy which they made, for their ministry, in imitation of Christ.

ADDENDA

A Note on the Translator

Steven S. Marshall is a specialist in the spiritual heritage of St. John Eudes. His book, *A Heart on Fire: St. John Eudes, Model of the New Evangelization,* has been translated into three languages and is sold worldwide. He blogs (doctorcordis.com) about spirituality. He is actively collaborating with the Vatican commission which is evaluating St. John Eudes as a candidate to be proclaimed a Doctor of the Church.

Steven S. Marshall

He holds a MA in Spiritual Theology from St. John's Seminary. Highest honors were awarded to his thesis: "Eudist Brothers: Living Communion Ecclesiology 'Before it was Cool.'" For a year he lived in Normandy, France as one of 15 people in a specialized program of spirituality studies. There, he walked in the footsteps of St. John Eudes and sat at the feet of spiritual masters from around the world. He now serves as translator and theologian for the US Region of the Eudists and lives with his wife in Southern California.

About St. John Eudes

Born in France on November 14, 1601, St. John Eudes' life spanned the "Great Century." The Age of Discovery had revolutionized technology and exploration; the Council of Trent initiated a much-needed reform in the Church; among the common people, it was the dawn of a golden age of sanctity and mystic fervor.

His Spiritual Heritage

No fewer than seven Doctors of the Church had lived in the previous century. Great reformers like St. Francis de Sales, St. Teresa of Avila, and St. John of the Cross had left an indelible mark on the Catholic faith. Their influence was still fresh as St. John Eudes came onto the scene.

He was educated by the Jesuits in rural Normandy. He was ordained into the Oratory of Jesus and Mary, a society of priests which had just been founded on the model of St. Philip Neri's Oratory in Rome. The founder was Cardinal Pierre de Bérulle, a man renowned for his holiness and named "the apostle of the Incarnate Word" by Pope Urban VII. Rounding out St. John Eudes' heritage is the influence of the Discalced Carmelites. His spiritual director, Cardinal Bérulle himself, had brought sisters from St. Teresa of Avila's convent to help found the Carmel in France. John Eudes would later become spiritual director to a Carmelite convent himself. Their cloister prayed constantly for his missionary activity.

His Life of Ministry

As an avid participant in a wave of re-evangelization in France, St. John Eudes' principal apostolate was preaching parish missions. Spending anywhere from 4 to 20 weeks in each parish, he preached over 120 missions across his lifetime, always with a team of confessors providing the sacrament around the clock, and catechists meeting daily with small groups of parishioners.

Early in his priesthood, an outbreak of plague hit St. John Eudes' native region and he rushed to provide sacraments to the dying. The risk of contagion was so great no one else dared to approach the victims. In order to protect his Oratorian brothers from contagion, St. John Eudes took up residence in a large empty cider barrel outside of the city walls until the plague had ended.

His Foundations

During his missions he heard countless confessions himself, including those from women forced into prostitution. Realizing that they needed intense healing and support, he began to found "Houses of Refuge" to help them get off the street and begin a new life. In 1641 he founded the Sisters of Our Lady of Charity of the Refuge to continue this work. They would live with the penitent women and provide them with constant support. Today, these sisters are known as the Good Shepherd Sisters, inspired by their fourth vow of zeal to go out seeking the "lost sheep."

Occasionally, St. John Eudes would return to the site of a previous mission. To his dismay, he found that the fruits of the mission were consistently fading for lack of support. The crucial piece in need of change was the priesthood. At that time, the only way to be trained as a priest was through apprenticeship. The result of this training was so horribly inconsistent that the term "hocus pocus" was invented during this time to describe the corrupted Latin used by poorly trained priests during the consecration at mass. In 1643 he left the Oratory and founded the Congregation of Jesus and Mary to create a seminary. Seminary training was a radical brand-new concept which had just been proposed by the Council of Trent.

His Mark on the Church

At a mission in 1648 St. John Eudes authored the first mass in history in honor of the Heart of Mary. In 1652 he built the first church under the Immaculate Heart's patronage: the chapel of his seminary in Coutances, France. During the process of his canonization, Pope St. Pius X named St. John Eudes "the father, doctor, and apostle of liturgical devotion to the hearts of Jesus and Mary." The Heart of Jesus because he created the first Feast of the Sacred Heart in 1672, just one year before St. Margaret Mary Alacoque had her first apparition of the Sacred Heart.

Although his Marian devotion was intense from a tender age, the primary inspiration for this feast came from St. John Eudes' theology of baptism. From the beginning of his missionary career he taught that Jesus continues His Incarnation in the life of each baptized Christian. As we give ourselves to Christ, our hands become His hands, our heart is transformed into His heart. Mary is the ultimate exemplar of this. She gave her heart to God so completely that she and Jesus have just one heart between them. Thus, whoever sees Mary, sees Jesus, and honoring the heart of Mary is never separate from honoring the heart of Jesus.

Doctor of the Church?

At the time of this writing, Bishops the world over have requested that the Vatican proclaim St. John Eudes as a Doctor of the Church. This would recognize his unique contribution to our understanding of the Gospel, and his exemplary holiness of life which stands out even among saints. For more information on the progress of this cause, on his writings or spirituality, or to sign up for our e-newsletter updates, contact spirituality@eudistsusa.org.

About the Eudist Family

During his lifetime, St. John Eudes' missionary activity had three major areas of focus.

- For priests, he provided formation, education, and the spiritual support which is crucial for their role in God's plan of salvation.
- For prostitutes and others on the margins of society, he gave them a home and bound their wounds, like the Good Shepherd with his lost sheep.
- For the laity, he preached the dignity of their baptism and their responsibility to be the hands and feet of God, to continue the Incarnation.

In everything he did, he burned with the desire to be a living example of the love and mercy of God.

These are the "family values" which continue to inspire those who continue his work. To paraphrase St. Paul, John Eudes planted seeds, which others watered through the institutions he founded, and God gave the growth. Today, the family tree continues to bear fruit:

The *Congregation of Jesus and Mary* (CJM), also known as The Eudists, continues the effort to form and care for priests and other leaders within the Church. St. John Eudes called this the mission of "teaching the teachers, shepherding the shepherds, and enlightening those who are the light of the world." Continuing his efforts as a missionary preacher, Eudist priests and brothers "audaciously seek to open up new avenues for evangelization," through television, radio, and new media.

The *Religious of the Good Shepherd* (RGS) continue outreach to women in difficult situations, providing them with a deeply needed place of refuge and healing while they seek a new life. St. Mary Euphrasia drastically expanded the reach of this mission which now operates in over 70 countries worldwide. A true heiress of St. John Eudes, St. Mary Euphrasia exhorted her sisters: "We must go after the lost sheep with no other rest than the cross, no other consolation than work, and no other thirst than for justice."

In every seminary and House of Refuge founded by St. John Eudes, he also established a *Confraternity of the Holy Heart of Jesus and Mary* for the laity, now known as the Eudist Associates. The mission he gave them was twofold: First, "To glorify the divine Hearts of Jesus and Mary... working to make them live and reign in their own heart through diligent imitation of their virtues." Second, "To work for the salvation of souls... by practicing, according to their abilities, works of charity and mercy and by attaining numerous graces through prayer for the clergy and other apostolic laborers."

The *Little Sisters of the Poor* were an outgrowth of this confraternity. St. Jeanne Jugan was formed as a consecrated woman within the Eudist Family. She discovered the great need for love and mercy among the poor and elderly and the mission took on a life of its own. She passed on to them the Eudist intuition that the poor are not simply recipients of charity, they provide an encounter with Charity Himself: "My little ones, never forget that the poor are Our Lord... In serving the aged, it is He Himself whom you are serving."

A more recent "sprout" on the tree was founded by Mother Antonia Brenner in Tijuana, Mexico. After raising her children in Beverly Hills and suffering through divorce, she followed God's call to become a live-in prison minister at the *La Mesa* penitentiary. The *Eudist Servants of the 11th Hour* was founded so that other women in the latter part of their lives could imitate her in "being love" to those most in need.

The example St. John Eudes set for living out the Gospel has inspired many more individuals and organizations throughout the world. For more information about the Eudist family, news on upcoming publications, or for ways to share in our mission, contact us at spirituality@eudistsusa.org.

Heart of the Holy Family: A Manual of Prayer

These are excerpts from *The Life and the Kingdom of Jesus: A Treatise on Christian Perfection for Use by Clergy or Laity*, translated from French by Thomas Merton in The Abbey of Our Lady of Gethsémani and published by Kennedy & Sons in New York, 1946.

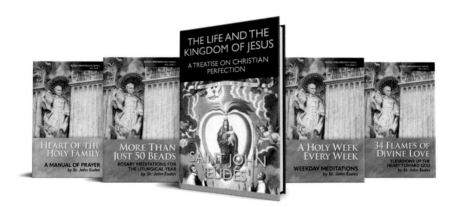

The Life and the Kingdom of Jesus as well as other titles in this series, *A Holy Week Every Week, More Thank Just 50 Beads* and *34 Flames of Divine Love* by St. John Eudes can be found in the Eudist bookstore on amazon.com.

More by Eudist Press

- *A Heart on Fire: St. John Eudes, a Model for the New Evangelization*
- *Spiritual Itinerary for Today with St. John Eudes*
- *Eudist Lectionary: A St. John Eudes Reader*

Eudist Prayerbook Series

- Volume 1: *Heart of the Holy Family:*
  A Manual of Prayer
- Volume 2: *More than Just 50 Beads:*
  Rosary Meditations for the Liturgical Year
- Volume 3: *A Holy Week Every Week:*
  Weekday Meditations
- Volume 4: *34 Flames of Divine Love:*
  Elevations of the Heart Towards God

Biography

- *St. John Eudes: Worker for the New Evangelization in the 17th Century*
- *In All Things, the Will of God: St. John Eudes Through His Letters*

More by St. John Eudes

St. John Eudes' Selected Works

- *The Life and Kingdom of Jesus in Christian Souls*
- *The Sacred Heart of Jesus*
- *The Admirable Heart of Mary*
- *The Priest: His Dignity and Obligations*
- *Meditations*
- *Letters and Shorter Works*

Other Works

- *Man's Contract with God in Holy Baptism*
- *The Wondrous Childhood of the Mother of God*

Made in the USA
Monee, IL
26 August 2020